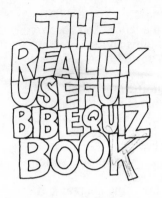

INTRODUCTION

NEW TESTAMENT

The purpose of this book is to provide some more *meaningful* questions for the Bible Quiz. While there are many quiz books and games based on the Bible, few attempt to deal with the great themes and real substance of the Bible. They are generally concerned with what you might call the "nuts and bolts" of it all — not that nuts and bolts are not important, it's just that what they hold together is **more** important.

So for instance, many quiz questions are more related to the trivial than the significant. "How many sons did Joktan have?" "How old was Peleg when he died?" "How many fish were in the net?" and so on. Perhaps it's because such answers have to be very precise. Names and numbers are either right or wrong. The problem is that they may not be too helpful to our Christian experience. Questions about the Bible should have one aim: to fix in our minds the glorious truths of God.

Questions then like "Who was the father of the sons of Zebedee?" have no place here! The aim is to concentrate on questions and answers that have some real *point* to them, rather than being so much trivia. Because the emphasis is on **meaning**, on the **sense** of the Bible and on the **intention** of revelation, the answers may be less precise, because you enter the area of interpretation. But if the purpose of making the Bible relevant and significant is to be pursued, then it cannot be otherwise.

For this reason the questions "why" and "how" are far more common. We are trying to look beyond the actual facts to explore the purpose, cause and motivation of the Biblical material. To know that Jesus used six stone jars in His miracle of turning water into wine is far less important than what He did and the reason why He did it!

Nor is it particularly helpful to know that the word "and" occurs over 46,000 times; or that a verse in Ezra contains all the letters of the alphabet except "j", or that Serug was 30 when his son Nahor was born.

The story is told of one lady who had committed the whole of the Bible to memory. She was tested, and could indeed recite any passage of Scripture at will. But when she was asked for its meaning, she could not answer. Rather like the Jews who searched the Scriptures, because as Jesus said, they thought that *in them* they had eternal life, not recognizing that it was these very Scriptures which testified of Jesus, *whom they did not know.*

So in this quiz book there are no requests for citing chapter and verse (although these are always given for reference). Nor are there any requirements for knowing the ages of the patriarchs, or the genealogy from David onwards. Nor is there any demand for reciting a particular verse word for word. It is the **sense** of the Bible passage that is all-important.

For this reason the questions are not particularly version-dependent. Nor should the questioner object if the answer given is not **exactly** as given on the card, since it should be clear whether the response is correct or not. In matters of dispute, defer to one another as in the Lord.

Also bear in mind that this exercise of increasing Bible knowledge is not a theological treatise. If a question sparks off a debate, that itself can be profitable! The questions have been kept within that core of what should be known to a good student of the Bible, generally avoiding texts that are unfamiliar or obscure. The purpose of Bible knowledge is not to demonstrate one's superiority, but to become more aware of all the many aspects of God's wonderful salvation *and to participate personally in that healing salvation.*

May the prime aim be that of the gospel message itself: to spread the good news about the wonderful God whose love and friendship we are privileged to have through this life, and in whose presence we are invited to spend all eternity.

JONATHAN GALLAGHER

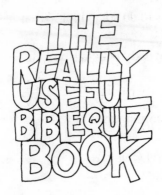

QUESTIONS

1. What does perfect love do? ✓ 1 JN. 4:18

2. In Romans 8:1, there is no condemnation for whom?

3. How did Jesus say that His disciples would be identified?

4. If it is only in this life we have hope in Christ, we are to be . . . what?

5. God is light, and in Him is no . . . what? ✓ 1 JN 1:5

6. What is the message of the cross to those who are perishing? ✓

7. Peter answered, "You are the Christ of God." What was the question? ✓

8. Jesus promised that whoever hears His word and believes in the one who sent Him would have . . . what? ✓

9. Why were the five foolish virgins foolish? ✓

10. Why do we know that when Jesus appears we shall be like Him?

11. If God is for us, then . . . ? · ROM. 8:31

12. What reason did Jesus give when He was asked why He ate with sinners? ✓

13. God is a spirit, so how is He to be worshipped? ✓

14. Jesus once healed a blind man. Why did the Pharisees complain? ✓

15. In Gethsemane Jesus asked His disciples to do something. What was it?

16. Why did Jesus say, "Take eat; this is my body which is broken for you"?

17. How can I "do all things"?   *PHILLIPIANS 4:13*

18. What happens to 'the dead in Christ' according to 1 Thessalonians?

19. Why does God call Himself the Alpha and Omega?

20. If anyone is in Christ, he (or she) is what?

21. How did God say His strength was made perfect?

22. Jesus said He hadn't come to destroy the Law or the Prophets, but to do what?

23. When Jesus spoke about prayer, what did He say **not** to do? *Mat 6:7*

24. If we brought nothing into this world, what else is certain?

25. When Jesus came to His own, what happened?

26. When Jesus referred to the saying 'An eye for an eye, and a tooth for a tooth', what did **He** say to do?

27. If a man looks at a woman with lust, what did Jesus say had happened?

28. For all have sinned and done what?

29. What does the true Light do?

30. Who was God and was in the beginning with God?

31. When Jesus was on the cross, He experienced the separation that sin brings, and it made Him cry out. What was this cry?

32. If Jesus is the vine, what are we to be?

33. Jesus promised that where two or three gathered together in His name He would do what?

34. Why did Jesus say to His disciples: "You are not all clean"?

35. When the disciples asked Jesus who was the greatest in the kingdom of heaven, Jesus replied that no one would enter the king-

dom of heaven unless they were . . . what?

36. Why did John "fall at his feet as though dead"?

37. Why did the angel ask the question: "Why are you standing here looking up to heaven?"

38. When Martha said that she knew her brother would rise again at the last-day resurrection, how did Jesus reply?

39. It's time to wake up from our spiritual slumber because our salvation is what?

40. What is the last enemy and what will happen to this enemy?

41. What happens to the living faithful when Jesus returns?

42. Since everything on this earth is to be destroyed, what kind of people ought we to be?

43. Why will there be no need for a lamp in New Jerusalem?

44. Once we were alienated from God and enemies in our minds because of our evil actions. But what has happened now?

45. What must we put on to stand against the Devil's weapons?

46. If the wage that sins pays is death, what in contrast does God promise?

47. According to Jesus, why do sheep not follow a stranger?

48. When Jesus told His fellow citizens in Nazareth that no prophet is honoured in his home country, what did they do?

49. Why did Jesus compare the time before His second coming to the days of Noah?

50. When Jesus asked the disciples if they wanted to leave Him too, what answer did He get?

51. What is the glorious appearing of our great God and Saviour, Jesus Christ, to be to the Christian?

52. Why does James say we have to control our tongue? JAMES 3: 5-8

53. How did God show His love to us?

54. When in the new earth we are God's people, and He is with us and is our God, what will He do?

55. Jesus promised to give us His peace. What kind of peace does He not give?

56. Why does Jesus say He will not pray to (plead) the Father for us?

57. Who is someone who says he loves God but hates his brother? 1JN4:20

58. What is the wage that sin pays?

59. Jesus told His disciples He no longer called them servants, but . . . what?

60. If Christ has not been raised from the dead, what is the result for Christians?

61. What was added because of transgression?

62. Why did Jesus say He was going to prepare a place for us?

63. In a moment, in the twinkling of an eye, at the last trumpet — what will happen?

64. Love does not delight in evil but in . . . what?

65. As in Adam all die, so in Christ . . . what?

66. Why did Paul call the Galatians foolish?

67. Now we see a poor reflection as in a mirror, but then what will we see?

68. Don't be deceived — God is not mocked. Why?

69. What did Jesus say would happen if He was "lifted up" from the earth?

70. What will the end-time "scoffers" be saying?

71. Why did those who claimed to be wise become fools?

72. Once we are justified (set right) by faith, what happens?

73. What is the answer to the question: "What must I do to be saved?" ACTS 16: 30, 31

74. What is eternal life, according to Jesus?

75. Why did Jesus say to one of the thieves crucified with Him, "You will be with me in Paradise"?

76. Jesus told Nicodemus that no one could see the kingdom of God unless . . . what?

77. In many and various ways God spoke in the past to our fathers through the prophets, but in these last days He has spoken how?

78. Philip asked Jesus to show them the Father. What was Jesus' response?

79. Why shouldn't people believe it when anyone says "Look! Here is Christ"?

80. I am not ashamed of the gospel; it is the power of God to do what?

81. Who was in Who reconciling the world to Himself?

82. John advises not to believe everyone who claims to have the Spirit, but to do what?

83. This is the record: Light came into the world, but men did what?

84. Jesus promised that if you know the truth, it will do something. What will it do?

85. The Law was put in charge of us (be our schoolmaster) to do what?

86. Why is the Lord patient (longsuffering) with us?

87. Why did Jesus say we would keep His commandments?

88. When the prodigal son came home, what did the father do immediately?

89. What did Jesus promise to all those who were burdened and heavily laden?

90. What is God's kindness meant to do?

91. Peter made a promise to Jesus that he didn't keep. What was it?

92. All things work together for good for who?

93. Why should we put on the armour of God?

94. But you, brothers, are not in darkness so that the day (of Christ's return) should not do what?

95. Why does Paul cry out: "What a wretched man I am! Who will

deliver me from this body of death?"

96. No man can have greater love than this. What is it?

97. Why are the merciful blessed?

98. What is Jesus' promise to anyone who hears His voice and answers His knock?

99. Foxes have holes, and birds have nests — but what does the son of man **not** have?

100. Why should you let your light shine before men?

101. What are these? Love, joy, peace, patience, kindness, goodness, faithfulness, gentleness and self-control? GAL . 5 : 22

102. What does Jesus promise to those who hunger and thirst after righteousness?

103. We are commanded by Jesus to go and teach all nations, and do what?

104. Why was falling asleep during one of Paul's sermons dangerous for one young man? ACTS 20 : 9

105. What did John the Baptist call the religious leaders who came out to see him?

106. Why did Peter say to Simon, "May your money perish with you"?

107. Why did Elizabeth's baby leap in her womb?

108. What did Jesus say was in His Father's house?

109. Why did Paul tell people to follow him?

110. Paul says that he has not obtained everything, nor has already been made perfect, but he does what?

111. Why did Jesus not turn the stones into bread as the tempter suggested?

112. Why did the crowd ask for Barabbas to be released?

113. What did Jesus say His present wicked generation asked for?

114. Why did Jesus give the "Lord's Prayer"?

115. What apparently good being can Satan transform himself into?

116. When Judas came up to Jesus to betray Him, what did Jesus say?

117. When Jesus came, He emptied Himself and took on what?

118. What did the woman do to find the lost coin?

119. "When I was a child, I spoke as a child, I understood as a child, I thought as a child," but then what?

120. What did the voice from the cloud on the mountain say to the disciples?

121. Why are the poor blessed?

122. When Jesus was crucified, He asked His Father to forgive His executioners. What reason did He give for His request?

123. Jesus sadly stated that to whoever denied Him before men, He would have to do what?

124. When Jesus was told of the death of John the Baptist, what did He do?

125. When Pilate asked the crowd if he should crucify their king, what was their reply?

126. Why did two thousand pigs drown themselves?

127. The disciples were terrified when they saw Jesus walking on the water to them. Why? Mk 6:49

128. When Jesus was asked whether He believed in paying the temple tax, why did He ask for a coin?

129. How do we know Jesus was really dead after He was crucified?

130. What did Jesus say would happen if He commanded the people not to praise God at His triumphal entry into Jerusalem?

131. Jesus humbled Himself, and became obedient — even to what?

132. Why did Jesus say to consider the lilies of the field?

133. Why did Jesus tell Thomas to touch His wounded hands and side?

134. What question did Jesus ask Peter three times? 21:15:17

135. What question did the Lord ask Saul on the road to Damascus?

136. What did Jesus say in answer to the question, "Who is my neighbour?"

137. What will be where your treasure is?

138. Instead of being drunk with wine, what should we be filled with?

139. Why did the dragon stand in front of the woman in Revelation?

140. Having put on the armour of God, what is our struggle against?

141. Why does Jesus say we should not be surprised if the world hates us?

142. What did Jesus say the widow had done when she put her two little coins into the temple treasury?

143. When the sun is darkened, and the moon does not give her light, and when the stars fall and the heavenly bodies are shaken — when these things happen what did Jesus say men would see?

144. What are we, even if we have faith that can move mountains and yet have no love?

145. When the Jews brought Jesus to Pilate and he asked what charges they were bringing against Jesus, how did they reply?

146. What is the treasure hid in a field that is so valuable that a man finding it will sell all he has to buy it?

147. Why did Ananias and Sapphira fall down dead?

148. When Paul and Barnabas brought the gospel to Lystra, how did the people react?

149. When Jesus described the devil, He said that from the beginning he was a what?

150. When Jesus healed the centurion's servant, what did He say about the centurion?

151. What did the passers-by say to Jesus as He hung on the cross?

152. How did Jesus say we are to love God? With all our what?

153. We are saved by grace through faith, and not . . . what?

154. Shall we go on sinning, so that . . . what?

155. If we seek first the kingdom of God and His righteousness, what will happen?

156. Jesus asked the question, "If we only love those that love us . . ." what then?

157. What were the first words of the angel to the shepherds at Bethlehem?

158. Why did the angel appear to Joseph in a dream?

159. Why did Jesus say "Take, eat" during His last Passover meal?

160. What was Jesus' declaration to the woman taken in adultery?

161. Why do we look for what is unseen, not what is seen?

162. What happens in heaven when one sinner repents?

163. When Jesus healed the ten lepers, what did He ask the one who returned?

164. When Pilate said to the crowd, "Here is the man," what did they reply?

165. What did the father do when he saw his prodigal son coming home?

166. What happened to the stone the builders rejected?

167. Jesus said, "I have come into the world as a light so that . . . what?"

168. When Jesus' attention was called to the temple buildings, how did He respond?

169. Why did the women wait until early Sunday morning before coming to anoint Jesus' body?

170. When the mob came out to Gethsemane with swords and sticks to arrest Jesus, what did He tell them?

171. How did the disciples walking on the road to Emmaus eventually recognize Jesus?

172. Why did John (in Revelation) weep when he saw the scroll?

173. Why did Jesus ask for a coin when asked about paying taxes?

174. What did the repentant thief ask Jesus on the cross?

175. Neither death nor life, neither angels nor demons . . . neither anything in all creation can do what?

176. After hearing Jesus say "How hard it is for the rich to enter the kingdom of God," His hearers asked "Who then can be saved?" What was Jesus' answer?

177. What are we not to repay?

178. Why did Jesus say, "Today salvation has come to this house"?

179. Once we were darkness, but now we are . . . what?

180. What question did the angels ask the women who came to Jesus' tomb?

181. Jesus is the image of the invisible God, and through Him all things . . . what?

182. Why did Jesus tell us to remember Lot's wife?

183. What did Jesus say to the woman healed by touching His cloak?

184. Why did the disciples in the boat worship Jesus?

185. Where is our citizenship (KJV: conversation)?

186. Jesus prayed: "Father, if it is your will, take this cup from me." What did He say next?

187. What kind of fight are we told to fight?

188. Jesus told a story of two men praying in the temple. What was the prayer of the one who went home justified before God?

189. If we died with Christ, we believe what?

190. Jesus asked a blind man at Jericho, "What do you want from me?" What did the man reply?

191. We are told: "Do not conform to the pattern of this world, but be . . ." what?

192. Why did Jesus say: "I have not found such faith in all of Israel"?

193. Paul writes: "The hour has come . . ." to do what?

194. Jesus said that only one sign would be given to His wicked

generation. What was it?

195. Where should every one be fully convinced?

196. Where is your life now hidden?

197. Jesus Christ is the same . . . when?

198. Jesus said that the Son of man did not come to be served, but to serve, and to do what?

199. "I tell you the truth," Jesus told the Jews, "Before Abraham was born . . ." what?

200. Why do we not look for a permanent (continuing) city here?

201. Jesus said He was the good shepherd. What did He say the good shepherd would do?

202. What serious accident followed by a miracle happened one Saturday night when Paul was preaching?

203. Why did Jesus say that whoever comes to Him would never go hungry?

204. What amazed Jesus about the faith in Nazareth?

205. Paul said that the sufferings of the present time are not worth comparing with what?

206. You are not your own, you were . . . what?

207. At the end-time, men will see the Son of man coming . . . how?

208. Jesus said: "Whoever hears my word and believes him who sent me has . . ." what?

209. All Scripture is given by inspiration of God, and is useful for . . . what?

210. Why did Jesus tell people not to believe it when anyone says "Look, here is the Christ!"?

211. What answer did Jesus give to the disciples of John the Baptist when they came asking if He was the Christ?

212. When Paul came to the Corinthians, he resolved to know nothing except what?

213. After He raised Jairus' daughter, what did Jesus ask for her?

214. As we grow up into Christ, how are we to speak the truth?

215. Who did Jesus say was His brother and sister and mother?

216. What did Paul say happened to him every day?

217. What did Jesus say would happen to whoever drinks the water He gives?

218. What did the voice from the cloud say on the Mount of Transfiguration?

219. What did Jesus say to do to them who hate you?

220. The foolishness of God is what?

221. When Jesus told His followers to look at the (spiritual) fields, what condition did He say they were in?

222. Why did Jesus say to His disciples, "Why are you so afraid? Have you no faith?"

223. What is in store for all who have fought the good fight, finished the race and kept the faith?

224. What is possible to him who believes?

225. What does Jesus say we have to take up if we are to be His disciple?

226. What does Jesus in Revelation say to those who have an ear?

227. What answer did Jesus receive to His question "John's baptism: was it from heaven, or from men?"?

228. Why did Paul refer to the inscription at Athens "To an Unknown God"?

229. When Jesus met Mary after His resurrection, what did He ask her?

230. What is the blessed hope we wait for as Christians?

231. When the prodigal son came home, what was the response of his older brother?

232. Why did the disciples say about Lazarus, "If he sleeps, he will get better"?

233. Like Paul, in what <u>one thing only</u> should we boast?

234. How audible will the coming of Jesus be?

235. Paul sent Onesimus back to Philemon, not as a slave but as what?

236. What did Jesus do as He walked with the two disciples on the road to Emmaus?

237. Why did Judas Iscariot complain about Mary's pouring expensive perfume on Jesus' feet?

238. Why did Jesus weep over Jerusalem?

239. We are saved by grace through faith, not of ourselves; it is the gift of God. It is not by works — why not?

240. What so astonished Paul about what was happening so quickly in the Galatian church that he had to write to them?

241. Today, if we hear His voice, what must we not do?

242. Why should we forgive everyone who sins (trespasses) against us?

243. Why is it time to wake up from our sleep?

244. How did Nicodemus react when Jesus told him, "You must be born again"?

245. What did Jesus tell the disciples when they argued over who was the greatest?

246. According to Jesus, even though heaven and earth would pass away, something would not . . . What?

247. What are we to do about things that are true, noble, right, pure, lovely, etc?

248. Who did Jesus say was not fit for service in the kingdom of God?

249. When Christ, who is your life, appears, then you also will . . . what?

250. Why was the rich young ruler upset with Jesus' advice to him?

251. Why have men loved darkness rather than light?

252. How did Jesus respond when the Pharisees told Him, "Teacher, rebuke your disciples"?

253. When the Lord returns from heaven at His second coming, how long will we be with Him?

254. Where is Christ now seated?

255. Why did the Pharisees complain about Jesus' disciples picking ears of corn?

256. When Jesus went into Jairus' daughter's room and said, "The child is not dead but asleep," what did the mourners do?

257. How bright did Jesus say His second coming would be?

258. What did Jesus say to the invalid who had been waiting by the pool for thirty-eight years?

259. Why is there neither Jew nor Greek, slave nor free, male nor female?

260. Whenever we eat the bread, and drink from the cup, we do what?

261. Why did Jesus say, "When all these things occur, stand up and lift up your heads"?

262. Jesus told the temple salesmen that instead of a house of prayer, they had made the temple what?

263. Eye has not seen, nor ear heard, nor has there entered into man's mind . . . what?

264. How will Jesus transform our lowly (vile) bodies?

265. Why did Jesus ask the question, "What is lawful on the Sabbath: to do good or to do evil, to save life or to kill?"?

266. Jesus said: "Whoever welcomes me does not welcome me but . . ." who?

267. What will the shield of faith do?

268. Compared to the incredible greatness of knowing Jesus, what did Paul count everything else?

269. When Jesus was asked about divorce, why did He say that Moses had allowed it?

270. When the dead in Christ are resurrected, what will happen to those "who are alive and remain"?

271. What question did the "rich young ruler" ask Jesus?

272. What kind of sinner did Paul call himself?

273. Why did Jesus tell us not to worry about what to wear?

274. James and John came to ask Jesus a special favour. What was it?

275. God did not appoint us to suffer wrath, but . . . what?

276. What is supposed to be buckled around our waists?

277. Through Jesus, how much did God reconcile to Himself?

278. Why are we to avoid foolish controversies and genealogies and arguments and quarrels about the law?

279. What are we told not to do with what God has joined together?

280. Who will come before the day of Christ (second coming)?

281. The law is not made for good men but who?

282. How did Jesus say we come to the Father?

283. The law is only a shadow of what?

284. Our fight is not against flesh and blood, but against what?

285. How did Jesus sum up the commandments?

286. When Philip asked Jesus to show them the Father, how did Jesus respond?

287. We shall not all sleep but we shall . . . what?

288. Why does Jesus pray to His Father that those whom the Father has given Him may be where He is?

289. Jesus promised to go and prepare a place for us. Why?

290. Jesus said, "It is not what goes into a man's mouth that makes him unclean, but . . ." what?

291. No one is what? — not even one.

292. What did the Good Samaritan say to the innkeeper?

293. What is the love of money?

294. What did Jesus tell the woman accused of adultery?

295. Why did Jesus say He must be lifted up as Moses lifted up the serpent in the wilderness?

296. What did Jesus say to the "little flock" that the Father would do?

297. Why did the angel tell Joseph to call Mary's son Jesus?

298. What did God say to the man in Jesus' parable who built bigger barns and laid up great stocks?

299. All have sinned and done what?

300. What power did Jesus give to all those who received Him and believed on His name?

301. We should not let the sun go down on our . . . what?

302. What question why did Jesus ask from the cross?

303. What did Jesus say will happen if you do not judge?

304. Jesus asked "What thanks do you have if you love . . ." who?

305. What should you seek first?

306. What happens to the one who knocks?

307. The wages of sin is death, but what is the gift of God?

308. In whom is there no truth?

309. For God so loved the world that He did what?

310. Jesus promised to be with His friends until when?

311. When Jesus told Pilate that everyone on the side of truth listened to Him, how did Pilate respond?

312. The word of God is quick and powerful and sharper than what?

313. In His parable, what did Jesus say should happen to the wheat and tares (weeds)?

314. What significant sign did Pilate have attached to Jesus' cross?

315. Why are those that mourn blessed?

316. When the Pharisees asked Jesus' disciples "Why does your teacher eat with tax collectors?", how did Jesus Himself reply?

317. Jesus promised that a time was coming when who would hear His voice?

318. Why are the pure in heart blessed?

319. Jesus said to His friends, "You are the light of the world." What did He say they were to do with that light?

320. We shall not all sleep, but we shall all be changed. How long will this take?

321. Perfect love drives out fear, because fear has to do with what?

322. John in Revelation saw a one like a son of man sitting on a cloud. What did He do?

323. What did the angels promise the disciples as they watched Jesus' ascension?

324. God did not send His Son into the world to condemn it, but to do what?

325. What is the sting of death?

326. What did Jesus say will happen to those who take up the sword?

327. Do not be drunk with wine, but be . . . what?

328. Nobody shall be justified in God's sight by what?

329. When the devil suggested to Jesus to end His hunger by turning stones into bread, how did Jesus respond?

330. What am I, even if I speak with the tongues of men and angels, and do not have love?

331. Pray without what?

332. Jesus said He would not drink of the fruit of the vine until when?

333. Great love has no man than what?

334. Unless a man is born again . . . what?

335. What does it profit a man if he gains the whole world, and . . . what?

336. What did Jesus do for us while we were still sinners?

337. Why did Jesus term the five foolish virgins foolish?

338. What did Herodias' daughter ask for?

339. Shall we go on sinning so that . . . what?

340. What did the mockers say to Jesus on the cross about His saving power?

341. Jesus told us that before picking out the speck from a brother's eye, we should do what?

342. Paul asked, "Who will rescue me from this body of death?" What was his conclusion?

343. Why did Jesus say it would be better for a man to have a millstone hung round his neck and be drowned?

344. What did Jesus say that God could do in response to the Jews' proud claim to be children of Abraham?

345. "Follow me," said Jesus, "and I will make you . . ." what?

346. When is the accepted time, when is the day of salvation?

347. What did the prodigal son say to his father on his return?

348. Why did Pilate say to the chief priests, "What I have written I have written"?

349. It is better to marry than to do what?

350. As Jesus was placed on the cross, what did He pray to His Father?

351. The good tidings of great joy that the angel announced to the shepherds were for whom?

352. What happened after the earthquake that followed Jesus' death?

353. Jesus said, "I did not come to call the righteous." What <u>did</u> He say He came for?

354. Why did Ananias and Sapphira fall down dead?

355. What did the centurion say about Jesus, having watched Him die?

356. When Simon Peter saw the great haul of fish that nearly broke their nets, what did he say?

357. Why do we look for new heaven, and a new earth, according to His promise?

358. What is the message that you have heard from the beginning — that we should do what?

359. Jesus told a story of two men owing money to a money-lender and having their debts cancelled. What question did Jesus end with?

360. Here is the patience of the saints, here are . . . who?

361. Why did the pigs rush into the lake and drown?

362. Jesus criticized the Pharisees in that they laid aside the commandments of God and did what?

363. Why was there great lamentations and weeping in symbolic "Rama"?

364. Why did the man in the parable go with joy and sell all he had?

365. Why do scoffers come, saying "Where is the promise of his coming?"

366. What are we to pray is done in earth as in heaven?

367. Stephen prayed, "Do not hold this sin against them". What sin?

368. Why did Jesus quote, "These people honour me with their lips, but their hearts are far from me?"

369. Jesus told His disciples, "Take, eat." What?

370. What was the visible sign of the Holy Spirit's outpouring at Pentecost?

371. What kind of temple is the Christian's body?

372. Why did Jesus say, "Who of you, if his son asks for some bread, gives him a stone?"?

373. For what reason shall a man leave his father and mother?

374. When the servants in the parable of the wheat and the tares (weeds) asked the owner where the tares had come from, what was his reply?

375. Why was Jesus disappointed with His disciples on His last visit to Gethsemane?

376. We know perfectly well that the day of the Lord comes . . . how?

377. Jesus said of the law that we were not to think He came to destroy, but . . . what?

378. If your brother has wronged you, what does Jesus say you should do first?

379. Why did the Father of the prodigal son say he wanted to celebrate his son's return?

380. When a woman recognized Peter as being one of Jesus' disciples after the arrest of Jesus, how did Peter reply?

381. Why were the disciples told to wait in Jerusalem after the ascension of Jesus?

382. What did Jesus say to John from the cross?

383. Why did Jesus say to lay up treasure in heaven?

384. What did Peter "give" to the lame man begging at the temple gate?

385. What does Paul say the sword of the Spirit is?

386. Do not be overcome by evil, but . . . what?

387. Why are the peacemakers blessed?

388. What will happen to those who are saying "Peace and safety"?

389. To show how much the Father cares for each of us, what did Jesus say are numbered?

390. In Revelation, what happens eventually to symbolic Babylon, representing the religion of the Anti-christ?

391. What do Christians show whenever they eat the bread and drink from the cup in Communion?

392. I can do all things . . . how?

393. What was Pilate's wife's advice to her husband about Jesus?

394. "If you do not believe I am the one I claim to be," said Jesus, "You will . . ." what?

395. When John in Revelation fell down to worship the angel, what was he told?

396. Jesus spoke about fleeing to the mountains, and to pray that your flight would not be when?

397. When Jesus identified Himself to the mob attempting to arrest Him, what happened to them?

398. What was the question Jesus asked Peter three times after His resurrection?

399. According to Jesus, how does the shepherd call his sheep?

400. Jesus gave His disciples a new commandment during His last supper on earth. What was it?

401. Christ must reign, until what is accomplished?

402. Awake sleeper, and arise from the dead, and . . . what?

403. What does Paul say happens to the consciences of those who leave the faith and speak lies?

404. Why does Jesus say the world will hate His disciples?

405. "Behold," says Jesus, "I come quickly; and . . ." what?

406. Why are the meek blessed?

407. Jesus told the Pharisees, "You have let go of the commandments of God and are holding on to the traditions of men." What was the question they asked Him?

408. It is recorded of the disciples that "They understood none of these things." What had Jesus tried to tell them?

409. What will happen to those who live godly lives in Christ Jesus?

410. When Jesus was about to heal the man let down through the roof, why did the scribes and Pharisees complain?

411. What shall be in the foreheads of the redeemed in the New Jerusalem?

412. Jesus told Thomas that because he had seen he had believed. Who were to be blessed?

413. What happens if we say we have so sin?

414. Jesus said, "Not everyone that says to me Lord, Lord, shall enter the kingdom of heaven, but . . ." who?

415. What did both Mary and Martha tell Jesus about Lazarus?

416. We implore (pray) you on Christ's behalf — to do what?

417. Where does the small gate and narrow road lead?

418. Why did Pilate wash his hands in front of the crowd?

419. Why did the chief priests want to kill Lazarus?

420. Jesus asked, "Can the blind lead the blind?" What was His conclusion?

421. Why did Jesus say "Don't cry" to a weeping mother?

422. Why will the redeemed in the New Jerusalem not need lamps or the light of the sun?

423. Christ has set us free, so we should stand firm and not let ourselves be burdened by what?

424. The Spirit Himself testifies with our spirit that we are what?

425. When Jesus after His resurrection appeared to His disciples behind locked doors, how did He greet them?

426. What was Pilate's first question to Jesus?

427. What did the voice from heaven say at Jesus' baptism?

428. What did King Agrippa think that Paul was trying to do to him?

429. Some early believers at Corinth were saying "I follow Paul"; or "I follow Apollos; and so on. What vital question did Paul then ask them?

430. Why will there be no more death or mourning or crying or pain?

431. Christ will appear the second time, not to bear sin, but to do what?

432. What lesson did Jesus tell us to learn from the fig tree?

433. John said he baptized with water, but the one who came after him would do what?

434. Why did the gaoler in Philippi draw his sword?

435. Jesus told His disciples, "I am the vine, you are . . ." what?

436. Jesus said: "Anyone who does not carry his cross and follow me cannot . . ." what?

437. One man promised Jesus, "I will follow you wherever you go." How did Jesus reply?

438. What trick question did the Sadducees ask Jesus, based on the fact they did not believe in a resurrection?

439. Jesus gave the figure of "seventy times seven". What was the question about?

440. Why did John the Baptist say, "Behold, the Lamb of God"?

441. According to James, what should no one say when they are tempted?

442. Why are we told by John to test the spirits?

443. Jesus told those who followed Him, "Unless you are converted and become like . . ." what?

444. According to Revelation, who will see Christ coming with the clouds?

445. Many are called, but . . . what?

446. Jesus explained to His disciples that He had told them to obey His commands and remain in His love so that . . . what?

447. Why did Judas at the end say he had sinned?

448. What did the people in the synagogue at Nazareth want to do to Jesus after He had preached?

449. We are told as Christians to have no debt except one. What?

450. What did Jesus say to Nicodemus that so amazed him?

451. What does Paul tell the Christians in Philippi that every tongue is to confess?

452. After Philip had explained the gospel to the eunuch, what did the eunuch want to do?

453. All things are pure to whom?

454. According to Jesus, no man can serve whom?

455. What does Jesus promise to do where two or three are gathered together in His name?

456. If someone keeps the whole law and yet breaks just one point what is the result?

457. What did one of the thieves crucified with Jesus ask Jesus to do for him?

458. It bears all things, believes all things, hopes all things, endures all things. What is it?

459. You will always have the poor with you, said Jesus. What would they **not** always have?

460. Paul says he would rather speak five words with understanding than what?

461. Why does Jesus tell His disciples that He no longer calls them servants?

462. What kind of giver does God love?

463. Jesus answered, "I am the way, the truth and the life." What was the question?

464. "All this I will give you," said the devil, "If you . . ." what?

465. What did John the Baptist not want to do for Jesus?

466. What does Paul in Corinthians say happened when he became a man?

467. Why didn't Jesus do many miracles in His home town?

468. For me to live is Christ, and . . . what?

469. When a woman was brought before Jesus accused of adultery, what did He do?

470. Why did Martha complain to Jesus?

471. We are to look to Jesus as the author and what of our faith?

472. What did Jesus say cannot add a single hour to your life?

473. Why were the Jews in Berea more noble than those in Thessalonica?

474. Three times Paul asked the Lord to take away something. What was it?

475. What according to Hebrews is the evidence (certainty) of what we do not see?

476. Why did Jesus say to Mary Magdalene, "Do not hold on to me"?

477. Paul wrote to the Christians in Corinth that God chose the foolish things of the world to do what?

478. Why did Jesus pronounce a blessing on the poor in spirit?

479. Why does God threaten to "spit" some professing Christians "out of His mouth"?

480. What sign did Judas give to identify Jesus as the one to be arrested?

481. What did Jesus say we should pray the Lord of the harvest for?

482. He that has the Son has life, but . . . what?

483. If we confess our sins, He is faithful and just to forgive us our sins and to do what?

484. What did Jesus say to the accusers of the woman caught in adultery?

485. According to Revelation the testimony of Jesus is what?

486. What is the meaning of "Immanuel"?

487. One Lord, one faith, one . . . what?

488. Jesus said, "You are the salt of the earth." But what did He say about salt that loses its saltiness?

489. Why did the labourers hired first to work in the vineyard grumble?

490. When Nathaniel heard where Jesus was from, what question did he ask?

491. According to Jesus, if He returns suddenly, do not let Him find you doing what?

492. What did Jesus say would happen to whoever could be trusted with very little?

493. How will Jesus respond to those who did not do God's will, but who claim to have prophesied and driven out demons and performed many miracles?

494. What do those Christians who say they are rich and need nothing not realize, according to the Revelation of Jesus?

495. Peter protested against Jesus' prediction of His crucifixion and resurrection. How did Jesus respond?

496. When Jesus' mother asked Him why He had remained behind in the temple, though He must have known they were searching for Him, how did Jesus reply?

497. "He that loves his father or mother more than me," said Jesus, is . . . what?

498. Speaking of the sheepfold, Jesus said, "I am the gate. Whoever enters through me shall . . ." what?

499. What does Paul tell the Romans he is not ashamed of?

500. Jesus says that He will not do something because the Father loves us Himself. What will He not do?

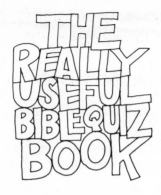

ANSWERS

1. *Casts out / drives out fear. (1 John 4:18.)*

2. *Those who are in Christ Jesus. (Romans 8:1.)*

3. *Because they would have love one for another. (John 13:35.)*

4. *Pitied more than all men. (Romans 15:19.)*

5. *Darkness at all. (1 John 1:5.)*

6. *Foolishness. (1 Corinthians 1:18.)*

7. *Who do you say that I am? (Luke 9:20.)*

8. *Eternal life. (John 5:24.)*

9. *Because they were running out of oil. (Matthew 25:8.)*

10. *Because we shall see Him as He is. (1 John 3:2.)*

11. *Who can be against us? (Romans 8:31.)*

12. *Because healthy people don't need a doctor, but the sick. (Matthew 9:11, 12.)*

13. *In spirit and in truth. (John 4:24.)*

14. *Because He healed Him on the Sabbath. (John 9:14.)*

15. *To keep watch (Mark 14:34.)*

16. *Because He wanted His followers to "do this in remembrance of me". (1 Corinthians 11:24.)*

17. "Through Christ who strengthens me". (Philippians 4:13.)

18. They shall rise first, [before all the faithful are translated].
(1 Thessalonians 4:16.)

19. Because He is the Beginning and the End, the one who is, and
who was, and who is to come. (Revelation 1.)

20. A new creature / creation. (2 Corinthians 5:17.)

21. In [man's] weakness. (2 Corinthians 12:9.)

22. To fulfil. (Matthew 5:17.)

23. Use vain repetitions. (Matthew 6:7.)

24. We'll carry nothing out. (1 Timothy 6:7.)

25. His own did not receive Him / did not welcome Him.
(John 1:11.)

26. Turn the other cheek etc. (Matthew 5:39.)

27. He had committed adultery with her in his heart (Matthew 5:28.)

28. Come short of the glory of God. (Romans 3:23.)

29. Lights everyone who comes into the world. (John 1:9.)

30. The Word. (John 1:1.)

31. "My God, my God, why have you forsaken me?" (Matthew
27:46.)

32. The branches. (John 15:5.)

33. Be there in the midst of them. (Matthew 18:20.)

34. Because He knew who was going to betray Him.
(John 13:10, 11.)

35. They were converted and became like little children. (Matthew
18:1, 3.)

36. He was overwhelmed by the brilliance of the vision of Christ.
(Revelation 1:13-16.)

37. Because the disciples were still gazing at the place where Jesus
had ascended. (Acts 1:10.)

38. *"I am the resurrection and the life . . ." (John 11:25.)*

39. *Nearer than when we first believed. (Romans 12:11.)*

40. *Death — will be destroyed. (1 Corinthians 15:26.)*

41. *Caught up in the clouds to meet the Lord in the air. (1 Thessalonians 4:17.)*

42. *We ought to live holy and godly lives [in view of the second coming]. (2 Peter 3:11.)*

43. *Because the Lord God will give them light. (Revelation 22:5.)*

44. *God has reconciled you through Christ and His death. (Colossians 1:21, 22.)*

45. *Put on the complete armour of God. (Ephesians 6:11.)*

46. *The gift of God is eternal life in Christ Jesus our Lord. (Romans 6:23.)*

47. *Because they do not recognize a stranger's voice. (John 10:5.)*

48. *Tried to throw Him off a cliff. (Luke 4:24, 29.)*

49. *Because people will be living in just the same way, without thought for their imminent end. (Matthew 24:37-39.)*

50. *Peter said, "Lord, who should we go to? You have the words of eternal life". (John 6:68.)*

51. *The blessed hope. (Titus 2:13.)*

52. *Because it makes great boasts, it is a fire, a poison, and can corrupt the whole person. (James 3:5-8.)*

53. *He sent His only son into the world that we might live through Him. (1 John 4:9; also John 3:16.)*

54. *He will wipe away every tear from their eyes. (Revelation 21:3, 4.)*

55. *The world's peace. (John 14:27.)*

56. *Because the Father loves you Himself. (John 16:26, 27.)*

57. *A liar. (1 John 4:20.)*

58. *Death. (Romans 6:23.)*

59. *Friends. (John 15:15.)*

60. *Preaching useless / faith useless / faith futile / still in sins (1 Corinthians 15:14, 17.)*

61. *The Law (Galatians 3:19.)*

62. *Because He wants us to be with Him (John 14:3.)*

63. *We will all be changed. (1 Corinthians 15:51, 52.)*

64. *Rejoices in the truth. (1 Corinthians 13:6.)*

65. *All will be made alive. (1 Corinthians 15:22.)*

66. *Because they were trying to achieve salvation by law-keeping and human effort. (Galatians 3:1-5.)*

67. *[God] Face to face. (1 Corinthians 13:12.)*

68. *Because a man reaps what He sows. (Galatians 6:7.)*

69. *He would draw all to Himself. (John 12:32.)*

70. *Where is the promise of His coming (for all things have continued from creation) (2 Peter 3:3, 4.)*

71. *Because instead of worshipping the immortal God they worshipped images made like men and animals and reptiles. (Romans 1:22, 23.)*

72. *We have peace with God through our Lord Jesus Christ. (Romans 5:1.)*

73. *"Believe on the Lord Jesus Christ and you shall be saved." (Acts 16:30, 31.)*

74. *"This is eternal life, that they know you, the only true God, and Jesus Christ whom you have sent." (John 17:3.)*

75. *Because the thief had asked Jesus to remember him when Jesus came into His kingdom. (Luke 23:42, 43.)*

76. *Unless he is born again. (John 3:3.)*

77. *By His Son. (Hebrews 1:1.)*

78. *"Anyone who has seen me has seen the Father." (John 14:8, 9.)*

79. *Because false Christs and false prophets will appear and work*

signs and wonders to try to deceive the elect. (Matthew 24:23, 24.)

80. Salvation to everyone who has faith / believes. (Romans 1:16.)

81. God in Christ. (2 Corinthians 5:19.)

82. Test them to see whether they come from God. (1 John 4:1.)

83. Loved darkness rather than light because their deeds were evil. (John 3:19.)

84. The truth will set you free. (John 8:32.)

85. To lead us to Christ. (Galatians 3:24, 25.)

86. Because He does not want any to perish, but all to come to repentance. (2 Peter 3:9.)

87. If we love Him. (John 14:15.)

88. Ran down the road to meet him and kissed him. (Luke 15:20.)

89. To give them rest. (Matthew 11:28.)

90. Lead you to repentance. (Romans 2:4.)

91. Never to deny Jesus. (Mark 14:31.)

92. Those who love God, those who are called according to His purpose. (Romans 8:28.)

93. To withstand the attacks of the Devil. (Ephesians 6:11.)

94. Surprise you like a thief. (1 Thessalonians 5:4.)

95. Because the good he wants to do he doesn't do, and the evil he doesn't want to do, he does! (Romans 7:24, 19)

96. To lay down his life for his friends. (John 15:13.)

97. For they shall obtain mercy. (Matthew 5:7.)

98. "I will come in to him and eat with him." (Revelation 3:20.)

99. Nowhere to lay His head. (Matthew 8:20.)

100. So that they might see your good works and glorify your Father in heaven. (Matthew 5:16.)

101. Fruits of the Spirit. (Galatians 5:22.)

102. They will be filled (satisfied). (Matthew 5:6.)

103. Baptize them in the name of the Father, Son and Holy Spirit. (Matthew 28:19.)

104. Because he fell out of the window he was sitting on. (Acts 20:9.)

105. A brood of vipers. (Matthew 3:7.)

106. Because Simon had wanted to buy the Holy Spirit. (Acts 8:18-20.)

107. Because of Mary's greeting. (Luke 1:41.)

108. Many rooms (mansions). (John 14:2.)

109. Because he followed Christ. (1 Corinthians 1:11.)

110. He presses on to take hold of that for which Christ Jesus took hold of him, towards the mark to win the prize. (Philippians 3:12, 14.)

111. Because He would have denied His mission, in that we are not to "live on bread alone, but on every word that comes out of the mouth of God". (Matthew 4:4.)

112. Because the chief priests and scribes told them to. (Matthew 27:20.)

113. Signs and wonders. (Luke 11:29.)

114. Because the disciples asked Him to teach them to pray. (Luke 11:1.)

115. An angel of light. (2 Corinthians 11:14.)

116. "Judas, are you going to betray the Son of man with a kiss?" (Luke 22:48.)

117. The form (nature) of a servant. (Philippians 2:7.)

118. Lit a lamp, swept the floor, and searched thoroughly until she found it. (Luke 15:8.)

119. When I became a man I put away childish things. (1 Corinthians 13:11.)

120. This is my Son, my chosen One; listen to Him. (Luke 9:35.)

121. *For theirs is the kingdom of God. (Luke 6:20.)*

122. *For they know not what they do. (Luke 23:34.)*

123. *Deny them before His Father in heaven. (Matthew 10:33.)*

124. *He went away by boat to be alone. (Matthew 14:13.)*

125. *We have no king but Caesar. (John 19:15.)*

126. *Because they were entered by evil spirits. (Mark 5:13.)*

127. *They thought He was a ghost. (Mark 6:49.)*

128. *Because it had the image of Caesar on it: rendering to Caesar what belongs to him. (Matthew 22:19-21.)*

129. *When the spear pierced His side, it brought out blood mixed with water. (John 19:34.)*

130. *Even the stones would cry out! (Luke 19:40.)*

131. *Death on a cross. (Philippians 2:8.)*

132. *Because they do not toil or spin, and yet are clothed by God — so do not worry. (Matthew 6:28-31.)*

133. *Because Thomas had said that unless he touched the actual wounds of Jesus, he would not believe. (John 20:25-27.)*

134. *Do you love me? (John 21:15-17.)*

135. *Why are you persecuting me? (Acts 9:4.)*

136. *He told the story of the Good Samaritan. (Luke 10:25-37.)*

137. *Your heart also. (Matthew 6:21.)*

138. *The Holy Spirit. (Ephesians 5:18.)*

139. *So that he might devour her child as soon as it was born. (Revelation 12:4.)*

140. *Rulers and powers of darkness; the spiritual forces of evil in heavenly places. (Ephesians 6:12.)*

141. *Because the world hated Him first, and we belong to Him. (John 15:18, 19.)*

142. *She had put in more than anyone else, because she gave out of*

her poverty all she had to live on. (Luke 21:4.)

143. The Son of man coming in the clouds with power and great glory. (Mark 13:24-26.)

144. Nothing. (1 Corinthians 13:2.)

145. They replied that if Jesus was not a criminal, they would not have brought Him to Pilate! (John 18:29, 30.)

146. The Kingdom of Heaven. (Matthew 13:44.)

147. Because they had dishonestly claimed to bring all the proceeds of a sale to the Church. (Acts 5:1-10.)

148. They said that the gods had come in human form and wanted to sacrifice to them. (Acts 14:11-18.)

149. A murderer. (John 8:44.)

150. That He had not found such a great faith in Israel. (Luke 7:9.)

151. Save yourself; come down from the cross if you are the Son of God. (Matthew 27:40.)

152. Heart, and soul, and mind. (Matthew 22:37.)

153. Of ourselves, it is the gift of God. (Ephesians 2:8.)

154. Grace may abound / increase? Certainly not! (Romans 6:1, 2.)

155. All these (other) things will be added to you. (Matthew 6:33.)

156. What reward will we have? (Matthew 5:46.)

157. Fear not / Do not be afraid. (Luke 2:10.)

158. Because he was planning to divorce Mary as she was expecting. (Matthew 1:19, 20.)

159. Because as He said, "This is my body", showing the need to be one with Him in Communion. (Matthew 26:26.)

160. Neither do I condemn you. Go and sin no more. (John 8:11.)

161. Because what is seen is temporary, what is unseen is eternal.

(2 Corinthians 4:18.)

162. There is rejoicing (joy). (Luke 15:10.)

163. *"Were not ten cleansed? Where are the other nine?" (Luke 17:17.)*

164. *"Crucify! crucify!" (John 19:6.)*

165. *He ran to his son, embraced him and kissed him. (Luke 15:20.)*

166. *It became the capstone / cornerstone. (Matthew 21:42.)*

167. *No one who believes in me should stay (abide) in darkness. (John 12:46.)*

168. *Not one stone will be left on another; all would be thrown down. (Mark 13:2.)*

169. *Because they were observing the Sabbath. (Luke 23:56; 24:1.)*

170. *"Am I a thief that you come to take me with swords and sticks? Wasn't I teaching every day in the temple, and you didn't arrest me then?" (Mark 14:48, 49.)*

171. *When He took bread, blessed and broke it. (Luke 24:30, 31.)*

172. *Because no one was able to open it. (Revelation 5:3, 4.)*

173. *To show it bore Caesar's image and name: and therefore to return to Caesar what are Caesar's, and to God what are God's. (Luke 20:25.)*

174. *To remember him when Jesus came in His kingdom. (Luke 23:42.)*

175. *Separate us from the love of God which is in Christ Jesus. (Romans 8:39.)*

176. *Things that are impossible with men are possible with God. (Luke 18:24-27.)*

177. *Evil for evil. (Romans 12:17.)*

178. *Because Zacchaeus had accepted Jesus and had promised to repay those he cheated. (Luke 19:8-10.)*

179. *Light in the Lord / Children of light. (Ephesians 5:8.)*

180. *"Why do you look for the living among the dead?" (Luke 24:5.)*

181. *Were created. (Colossians 1:15, 16.)*

182. To remind us not to look back, especially on the last day. (Luke 17:30-32.)

183. Your faith has healed you (made you whole). Go in peace. (Luke 8:48.)

184. Because they believed He was the Son of God in that He had stilled the wind and the waves. (Matthew 14:32, 33.)

185. In heaven. (Philippians 3:20.)

186. Yet not my will but yours be done. (Luke 22:42.)

187. The good fight of faith. (1 Timothy 6:12.)

188. "God have mercy on me, a sinner." (Luke 18:10-14.)

189. We will also live with Him. (Romans 6:8.)

190. "Lord, I want to see." (Luke 18:35-43.)

191. "Be transformed by the renewing of your mind." (Romans 12:2.)

192. Because of the centurion's trust in Jesus' ability to heal his servant. (Matthew 8:7-10.)

193. To wake up from your sleep. (Romans 13:11.)

194. The sign of Jonah. (Luke 11:29.)

195. In his own mind. (Romans 14:5.)

196. With Christ in God. (Colossians 3:3.)

197. Yesterday, today and forever. (Hebrews 13:8.)

198. To give His life as a ransom for many. (Mark 10:45.)

199. "I am". (John 8:58.)

200. Because we are looking for the city that is to come. (Hebrews 13:14.)

201. Lay down His life for the sheep. (John 10:7.)

202. A young man (Eutychus) went to sleep and fell from a third floor window. He was picked up dead, but revived by Paul. (Acts 20:7-12.)

203. Because He is the bread of life. (John 6:35.)

204. The lack of it! (Mark 6:6.)

205. The glory that shall be revealed in us. (Romans 8:18.)

206. Bought with a price. (1 Corinthians 6:19, 20.)

207. In clouds with great power and glory. (Mark 13:26.)

208. Everlasting life. (John 5:24.)

209. Doctrine (teaching), reproof, correction and instruction in righteousness. (2 Timothy 3:16.)

210. Because false christs and prophets would appear performing signs and miracles. (Mark 13:21, 22.)

211. "Go back and tell John what you have seen and heard" — the miracles etc. (Luke 7:18-22.)

212. Jesus Christ and Him crucified. (1 Corinthians 2:2.)

213. He asked that they give her something to eat. (Mark 5:42, 43.)

214. In love. (Ephesians 4:15.)

215. Whoever does God's will. (Mark 3:35.)

216. He died! (1 Corinthians 15:31.)

217. They would never thirst again. (John 4:14.)

218. "This is my beloved Son: listen to him." (Mark 9:7.)

219. Do good to them. (Luke 6:27.)

220. Wiser than man's wisdom. (1 Corinthians 1:25.)

221. Ready (white) to harvest. (John 4:35.)

222. Because they woke Him as He slept in the boat, fearing that the storm would drown them. (Mark 4:35-41.)

223. A crown of righteousness. (2 Timothy 4:7, 8.)

224. Everything. (Mark 9:23.)

225. Take up our cross. (Luke 14:26.)

226. Let him hear. (Revelation 2:7, etc.)

227. *"We cannot tell" ("We don't know") (Mark 11:30, 33.)*

228. *Because he wanted to reveal and tell them about this "unknown" God. (Acts 17:23.)*

229. *"Woman, why are you crying?" (John 20:15.)*

230. *"The glorious appearing of our great God and Saviour, Jesus Christ. (Titus 2:13.)*

231. *He was angry (at the expense and celebration for his younger brother). (Luke 15:25-32.)*

232. *Because they did not realize that Jesus meant that Lazarus was dead. (John 11:12.)*

233. *The cross of Christ. (Galatians 6:14.)*

234. *Very! — with a shout, the voice of the archangel and the trumpet call of God. (1 Thessalonians 4:16.)*

235. *A dear brother in the Lord. (Philemon 16.)*

236. *Explained to them the scriptures concerning Himself. (Luke 24:27.)*

237. *Because he was a thief, and would have wanted the perfume sold so he could benefit. (John 12:5, 6.)*

238. *Because the people were not willing to come to Him (repent and be saved). (Matthew 23:37.)*

239. *So that no one can boast. (Ephesians 2:8, 9.)*

240. *That they were turning to a different "gospel" (of legalism). (Galatians 1:6, 7.)*

241. *Harden our hearts. (Hebrews 3:7, 8.)*

242. *Because we expect God to forgive us. (Luke 11:4.)*

243. *Because our salvation is nearer now than when we first believed. (Romans 13:11, 12.)*

244. *"How can a man be born when he is old? Surely he cannot enter his mother's womb a second time?" (John 3:3, 4.)*

245. *If anyone wants to be first, he must be the very last, and the servant of all. (Mark 9:35.)*

246. *His words. (Mark 13:31.)*

247. *Think on these things. (Philippians 4:8.)*

248. *He who puts his hand to the plough and looks back. (Luke 9:62.)*

249. *Appear with Him in glory. (Colossians 3:4.)*

250. *Because he was very wealthy (and probably wanted to stay that way). (Mark 10:22.)*

251. *Because their deeds were evil. (John 3:19.)*

252. *"I tell you, if they keep quiet, the stones will cry out." (Luke 19:39, 40.)*

253. *Forever. (1 Thessalonians 4:17.)*

254. *At the right hand of God. (Colossians 3:1.)*

255. *Because they were doing this on the Sabbath day. (Mark 2:23, 24.)*

256. *Laughed at Him. (Mark 5:38-40.)*

257. *Like lightning flashing from the east to the west. (Luke 17:24.)*

258. *Get up, take up your bed, and walk. (John 5:8.)*

259. *Because we are all one in Christ Jesus. (Galatians 3:28.)*

260. *Proclaim the Lord's death until He comes. (1 Corinthians 11:26.)*

261. *Because "your redemption is drawing near." (Luke 21:28.)*

262. *"A den of thieves." (Luke 19:46.)*

263. *What God has prepared for those who love Him. (1 Corinthians 2:9.)*

264. *So that they will be like His glorious body. (Philippians 3:21.)*

265. *Because some of the legalists were looking for a reason to accuse Jesus. (Mark 3:1-4.)*

266. *The one who sent me. (Mark 9:37.)*

267. *Put out all the flaming arrows (darts) of the evil one. (Ephesians 6:16.)*

268. *Loss / rubbish. (Philippians 3:8.)*

269. *Because of the hardness of their hearts. (Mark 10:5.)*

270. *They will be caught up together with the resurrected dead in Christ to meet the Lord in the air. (1 Thessalonians 4:17.)*

271. *"What must I do to inherit eternal life?" (Mark 10:17.)*

272. *The chief / the worst. (1 Timothy 1:15.)*

273. *Because God will clothe us as He does the flowers. (Matthew 6:28-30.)*

274. *For one to sit on the right and the other on the left in Jesus' glory (i.e. His kingdom). (Mark 10:35-37.)*

275. *To receive salvation through our Lord Jesus Christ. (1 Thessalonians 5:9.)*

276. *The belt of truth. (Ephesians 6:14.)*

277. *All things, whether things on earth or things in heaven. (Colossians 1:20.)*

278. *Because these are unprofitable and useless (vain). (Titus 3:9.)*

279. *Not to separate (put asunder). (Mark 10:9.)*

280. *The man of sin / lawlessness (Anti-Christ). (2 Thessalonians 2:3.)*

281. *Lawbreakers and rebels, ungodly and sinful etc. (1 Timothy 1:9, 10.)*

282. *Through Him. (John 14:6.)*

283. *The good things to come. (Hebrews 10:1.)*

284. *Rulers and authorities and powers of this dark world, and against the spiritual forces of evil in the heavenly realms. (Ephesians 6:12.)*

285. *Love the Lord and love your neighbour as yourself. (Mark 12:30, 31.)*

286. *He that has seen me has seen the Father. (John 14:8, 9.)*

287. *Be changed. (1 Corinthians 15:51.)*

288. *So that they may behold His glory. (John 17:24.)*

289. *So that when He comes again He can take us to be with Him. (John 14:2, 3.)*

290. *What comes out of his mouth. (Matthew 15:11.)*

291. *Righteous. (Romans 3:10.)*

292. *"Look after him (the man robbed and injured) and when I come back I'll pay any extra owing." (Luke 10:35.)*

293. *The root of all evil. (1 Timothy 6:10.)*

294. *"Neither do I condemn you; go and sin no more." (John 8:11.)*

295. *"So that whosoever believed in him should not perish, but have eternal life." (John 3:15.)*

296. *Give them the kingdom. (Luke 12:32.)*

297. *Because He shall save His people from their sins. (Matthew 1:21.)*

298. *You fool, this night your soul is required of you — then whose will all these things be? (Luke 12:20.)*

299. *Come short of the glory of God. (Romans 3:23.)*

300. *Power to become the sons of God. (John 1:12.)*

301. *Wrath / anger. (Ephesians 4:26.)*

302. *My God, my God, why have you forsaken me? (Matthew 28:46.)*

303. *You will not be judged. (Luke 6:37.)*

304. *Those who love you. (Luke 6:32.)*

305. *The kingdom of God and His righteousness. (Matthew 6:33.)*

306. *The door will be opened. (Matthew 7:8.)*

307. *Eternal life through Jesus Christ our Lord. (Romans 6:23.)*

308. *The devil. (John 8:44.)*

309. *Gave His one and only Son. (John 3:16.)*

310. *The end of the world. (Matthew 28:20.)*

311. *Pilate asked "What is truth?" and left. (John 18:37, 38.)*

312. *Any two-edged sword. (Hebrews 4:12.)*

313. *Let them grow together until harvest, to be separated only then. (Matthew 13:30.)*

314. *Jesus of Nazareth, King of the Jews. (John 19:19.)*

315. *For they shall be comforted. (Matthew 5:4.)*

316. *It's not the healthy that need a doctor, but the sick. (Matthew 9:11, 12.)*

317. *All who are in their graves. (John 5:28.)*

318. *For they shall see God. (Matthew 5:8.)*

319. *To let it shine before men that they might glorify God. (Matthew 5:14-16.)*

320. *In a moment, in the twinkling of an eye. (1 Corinthians 15:51, 52.)*

321. *Punishment. (1 John 4:18.)*

322. *Harvest the earth. (Revelation 14:14-16.)*

323. *"This same Jesus" would come as they had seen Him go. (Acts 1:11.)*

324. *To save the world through Him (Jesus). (John 3:17.)*

325. *Sin. (1 Corinthians 15:56.)*

326. *They will die by the sword. (Matthew 26:52.)*

327. *Filled with the Spirit. (Ephesians 5:18.)*

328. *Observing the Law. (Romans 3:20.)*

329. *Man shall not live by bread alone, but by every word that comes from the mouth of God. (Matthew 4:4.)*

330. *A sounding gong or clashing cymbal. (1 Corinthians 13:1.)*

331. *Ceasing. (1 Thessalonians 5:17.)*

332. *The kingdom of God comes. (Luke 22:18.)*

333. *That he lay down his life for his friends. (John 15:13.)*

334. *He cannot see the kingdom of God. (John 3:3.)*

335. *Loses his own soul. (Matthew 16:26.)*

336. *Died for us. (Romans 5:8.)*

337. *Because they brought no oil with them to wait. (Matthew 25:2, 3.)*

338. *The head of John the Baptist. (Mark 22-24.)*

339. *Grace may abound / increase. (Romans 6:1.)*

340. *He saved others; let Him save Himself / He cannot save Himself. (Luke 23:35; Matthew 27:42.)*

341. *Take the beam out of our own eye. (Matthew 7:5.)*

342. *"Thanks be to God — through Jesus Christ our Lord!" (Romans 7:25.)*

343. *Because this would be better than to cause a child to stumble. (Matthew 18:6.)*

344. *God could raise up children of Abraham from the stones. (Luke 3:8.)*

345. *Fishers of men. (Matthew 4:19.)*

346. *Now! (2 Corinthians 6:2.)*

347. *I have sinned against heaven and against you. I am no longer worthy to be called your son. (Luke 15:21.)*

348. *Because they were complaining about the sign Pilate had placed on Jesus' cross. (John 19:21, 22.)*

349. *Burn (with passion). (1 Corinthians 7:9.)*

350. *Father forgive them, for they don't know what they're doing. (Luke 23:34.)*

351. *All people. (Luke 2:10.)*

352. *The graves were opened and the bodies of many saints were resurrected. (Matthew 27:51, 52.)*

353. *To call sinners to repentance. (Luke 5:32.)*

354. *Because they were discovered defrauding and lying to God.*

(Acts 5:1-11.)

355. Surely this man was the son of God. (Mark 15:39.)

356. "Get away from me, Lord; I am a sinful man." (Luke 5:8.)

357. Because that is where righteousness dwells. (2 Peter 3:13.)

358. Love one another. (1 John 3:11.)

359. "Which one of them will love him more?" (Luke 7:42.)

360. Those that keep the commandments of God and the faith of Jesus. (Revelation 14:12.)

361. Because the devils entered them. (Luke 8:33.)

362. Held on to the traditions of men. (Mark 7:8.)

363. Because Herod had killed all the infants in Bethlehem. (Matthew 2:16-18.)

364. To buy the field with the hidden treasure. (Matthew 13:44.)

365. Because it seems that all things continue as they were since the beginning of creation. (2 Peter 3:3, 4.)

366. God's will. (Luke 11:2.)

367. The sin of stoning him to death. (Acts 7:60.)

368. Because the hypocritical Pharisees made a show of honouring God but they were intent on trapping Jesus. (Matthew 15:7-9.)

369. The bread, symbolic of Jesus' body. (Matthew 26:26.)

370. Tongues like fire. (Acts 2:1-4.)

371. The temple of the Holy Spirit in you. (1 Corinthians 6:19.)

372. Because if even evil human beings give good things to their children, how much more will our heavenly Father give good things to those who ask Him. (Matthew 7:11.)

373. To marry (to be united to his wife and the two become one flesh). (Matthew 19:5.)

374. An enemy has done this. (Matthew 13:27, 28.)

375. Because they fell asleep and could not keep Him company.

(Luke 22:46.)

376. Like a thief in the night. (1 Thessalonians 5:2.)

377. To fulfil. (Matthew 5:17.)

378. Go and speak to him in private. (Matthew 18:15.)

379. "For this my son was dead, and is alive again; he was lost, and is found." (Luke 15:24.)

380. "Woman, I don't know him." (Luke 22:57.)

381. They were told to wait until they received power from on high. (Luke 24:49.)

382. "Here is your mother", (referring to Mary, Jesus' mother). (John 19:27.)

383. For where your treasure is, there will your heart be too. (Matthew 6:20, 21.)

384. In the name of Jesus he "gave" him not silver or gold but the gift of healing — he walked. (Acts 3:6, 7.)

385. The word of God. (Ephesians 6:17.)

386. Overcome evil with good. (Romans 12:21.)

387. For they shall be called the children (sons) of God. (Matthew 5:9.)

388. Sudden destruction (at the second coming). (1 Thessalonians 5:3.)

389. The very hairs of your head. (Matthew 10:30.)

390. It falls. (Revelation 18:2.)

391. They "show the Lord's death until he comes". (1 Corinthians 11:26.)

392. Through Christ who strengthens me. (Philippians 4:13.)

393. "Have nothing to do with that innocent man." (Matthew 27:19.)

394. Die in your sins. (John 8:24.)

395. Don't do it; worship God. (Revelation 19:10.)

396. In winter or on the Sabbath day. (Matthew 24:20.)

397. They drew back and fell to the ground. (John 18:5, 6.)

398. "Simon, son of Jonas, do you love me?" (John 21:15-17.)

399. By name. (John 10:3.)

400. Love one another as I have loved you. (John 13:34.)

401. Until He has put all enemies under His feet. (1 Corinthians 15:25.)

402. Christ shall give you light. (Ephesians 5:14.)

403. Their consciences are seared with a hot iron. (1 Timothy 4:2.)

404. Because they do not belong to the world; Jesus has chosen them out of the world. (John 15:19.)

405. My reward is with me, and I will give to everyone according to what they have done. (Revelation 22:12.)

406. For they shall inherit the earth. (Matthew 5:5.)

407. "Why don't your disciples live according to the tradition of the elders?" (especially in regard to eating and ceremonial uncleanness). (Mark 7:5, 8.)

408. About His suffering, death and resurrection. (Luke 18:31-34.)

409. They shall suffer persecution. (2 Timothy 3:12.)

410. Because Jesus said, "Man, your sins are forgiven you" — which the Pharisees thought was blasphemy. (Luke 5:20, 21.)

411. God's name. (Revelation 22:4.)

412. Those who have not seen and yet have believed. (John 20:29.)

413. We deceive ourselves, and the truth is not in us. (1 John 1:8.)

414. He that does the will of my Father in heaven. (Matthew 7:21.)

415. Lord, if you had been here my brother would not have died. (John 11:21, 32.)

416. Be reconciled to God. (2 Corinthians 5:20.)

417. To life. (Matthew 7:14.)

418. In a vain attempt to show himself guiltless in the matter of

Jesus' execution. (Matthew 27:24.)

419. Because many people believed in Jesus because of His resurrection of Lazarus. (John 12:10, 11.)

420. "Won't they both fall into a ditch?" (Luke 6:39.)

421. Because He was about to resurrect her son. (Luke 7:11-15.)

422. Because the Lord God will give them light. (Revelation 22:5.)

423. The yoke of slavery (of trying to achieve salvation through the law). (Galatians 5:1.)

424. God's children. (Romans 8:16.)

425. "Peace be with you!" (John 20:19.)

426. "Are you the king of the Jews?" (Matthew 27:11.)

427. You are my beloved son; with you am I well pleased. (Luke 3:22.)

428. Convert him to Christianity. (Acts 26:28.)

429. Is Christ divided? (1 Corinthians 1:12, 13.)

430. For the old order of things (former things) has passed away. (Revelation 21:4.)

431. To bring salvation to those who are waiting for Him. (Hebrews 9:28.)

432. That as the sprouting of leaves show summer is near, so the signs of the times show Christ's coming is near. (Matthew 24:32, 33.)

433. Baptize with the Holy Spirit. (Mark 1:8.)

434. Because he was about to kill himself, thinking that his prisoners had escaped. (Acts 16:27.)

435. The branches. (John 15:5.)

436. "Be my disciple." (Luke 14:27.)

437. Foxes have holes, and birds of the air have nests, but the Son of Man has nowhere to lay his head." (Luke 9:57, 58.)

438. Whose wife would a woman be if she married seven brothers in turn, each of whom died. *(Matthew 22:23-28.)*

439. How many times to forgive your brother. *(Matthew 18:21, 22.)*

440. Because he saw Jesus passing by. *(John 1:35.)*

441. "God is tempting me". *(James 1:13.)*

442. To see whether they are from God. *(1 John 4:1.)*

443. Little children. *(Matthew 18:3.)*

444. Every eye shall see Him, even those who pierced Him. *(Revelation 1:7.)*

445. Few are chosen. *(Matthew 22:14.)*

446. His joy would remain in them and that their joy would be complete. *(John 15:9-11.)*

447. Because he had betrayed innocent blood. *(Matthew 27:4.)*

448. Throw Him off a cliff. *(Luke 4:20-29.)*

449. The "debt" of loving one another. *(Romans 13:8.)*

450. You must be born again. *(John 3:3-7.)*

451. That Jesus Christ is Lord. *(Philippians 2:11.)*

452. To be baptized. *(Acts 8:35, 36.)*

453. The pure. *(Titus 1:15.)*

454. Two masters. *(Matthew 6:24.)*

455. To be there in the midst of them. *(Matthew 18:20.)*

456. He is guilty of all. *(James 2:10.)*

457. To remember him when Jesus came into His kingdom. *(Luke 23:42.)*

458. Love (charity). *(1 Corinthians 13:7.)*

459. Jesus Himself. *(John 12:8.)*

460. Ten thousand words in a tongue. *(1 Corinthians 14:19.)*

461. Because a servant does not know his master's business *(unlike a friend). (John 15:15.)*

462. *A cheerful giver. (2 Corinthians 9:7.)*

463. *"How can we know the way?" (John 14:6.)*

464. *If you will bow down and worship me. (Matthew 4:9.)*

465. *Baptize Him. (Matthew 3:13, 14.)*

466. *He put away childish things. (1 Corinthians 13:11.)*

467. *Because of their lack of faith. (Matthew 13:58.)*

468. *To die is gain. (Philippians 1:21.)*

469. *Write in the dust. (John 8:6, 8.)*

470. *Because she wanted her sister Mary to help her with her preparations. (Luke 10:38-40.)*

471. *Finisher (perfecter). (Hebrews 12:2.)*

472. *Worry. (Matthew 6:27.)*

473. *Because they received the word readily and searched the scriptures daily to see whether those things were so. (Acts 17:11.)*

474. *His "thorn in the flesh" (some medical problem?).*
(2 Corinthians 12:8.)

475. *Faith. (Hebrews 11:1.)*

476. *Because He had not yet ascended to His Father. (John 12:17.)*

477. *To confound (shame) the wise. (1 Corinthians 1:27.)*

478. *Because theirs is the kingdom of heaven. (Matthew 5:3.)*

479. *Because they are only lukewarm, neither hot nor cold. (Revelation 3:16.)*

480. *A kiss. (Matthew 26:48, 49.)*

481. *To send workers (labourers) into His harvest fields. (Matthew 9:38.)*

482. *He that does not have the Son does not have life. (1 John 5:12.)*

483. *Cleanse us from all unrighteousness. (1 John 1:9.)*

484. *Whoever is without sin among you, cast the first stone. (John 8:7.)*

485. The spirit of prophecy. (Revelation 19:10.)

486. God with us. (Matthew 1:23.)

487. Baptism. (Ephesians 4:5.)

488. It was good for nothing except to be thrown away. (Matthew 5:13.)

489. Because they expected to be paid more than those who only worked an hour. (Matthew 20:11, 12.)

490. Can any good thing come out of Nazareth? (John 1:46.)

491. Sleeping. (Mark 13:36.)

492. They could be trusted with much. (Luke 16:10.)

493. I never knew you. Depart from me, you evil doers. (Matthew 7:21-23.)

494. They do not realize that they are poor, and blind and naked! (Revelation 3:17.)

495. Get behind me, Satan! (Matthew 16:22.)

496. Why were you searching for me? Didn't you know I had to be about my Father's business? (Luke 2:48, 49.)

497. Not worthy of me. (Matthew 10:37.)

498. Be saved. (John 10:9.)

499. The gospel. (Romans 1:16.)

500. Ask (pray) the Father on our behalf. (John 16:26, 27.)